THIS BOOK
BELONGS TO

THANK YOU!
FOR ANY SUGGESTIONS
OR IF YOU WANT TO BE NOTIFIED
WHEN NEW BOOKS ARRIVE YOU
CAN NOTIFY US ON :
MY.MAIL6510@GMAIL.COM

www.ingramcontent.com/pod-product-compliance
Lightning Source LLC
Chambersburg PA
CBHW081315250726
48662CB00008B/2582